W9-DCG-735

BEARS

alex kuskowski

Consulting Editor, Diane Craig,
M.A./Reading Specialist

Sandcastle

An Imprint of Abdo Publishing
www.abdopublishing.com

visit us at www.abdopublishing.com

Published by Abdo Publishing, a division of ABDO, PO Box 398166, Minneapolis, Minnesota 55439.
Copyright © 2015 by Abdo Consulting Group, Inc. International copyrights reserved in all countries.
No part of this book may be reproduced in any form without written permission from the publisher.
SandCastle™ is a trademark and logo of Abdo Publishing.

Printed in the United States of America, North Mankato, Minnesota
062014
092014

Editor: Liz Salzmann
Content Developer: Nancy Tuminelly
Cover and Interior Design: Anders Hanson, Mighty Media, Inc.
Photo Credits: Shutterstock

Library of Congress Cataloging-in-Publication Data
Kuskowski, Alex., author.
  Bears / Alex Kuskowski.
     pages cm. -- (Zoo animals)
  Audience: 004-009.
  ISBN 978-1-62403-271-4
1. Bears--Juvenile literature. I. Title.
  QL737.C27K826 2015
  599.78--dc23
                              2013041826

SandCastle™ Level: Transitional

SandCastle™ books are created by a team of professional educators, reading specialists, and content developers around five essential components—phonemic awareness, phonics, vocabulary, text comprehension, and fluency—to assist young readers as they develop reading skills and strategies and increase their general knowledge. All books are written, reviewed, and leveled for guided reading, early reading intervention, and Accelerated Reader® programs for use in shared, guided, and independent reading and writing activities to support a balanced approach to literacy instruction. The SandCastle™ series has four levels that correspond to early literacy development. The levels are provided to help teachers and parents select appropriate books for young readers.

EMERGING · BEGINNING · **TRANSITIONAL** · FLUENT

CONTENTS

BEARS

Bears are big **mammals.**

People see bears at the zoo.

AT THE ZOO

Bears at the zoo live in a pen. They have trees. They have water. They have toys.

BEAR FEATURES

Bears have thick fur.
Their fur can be
white, brown,
or black.

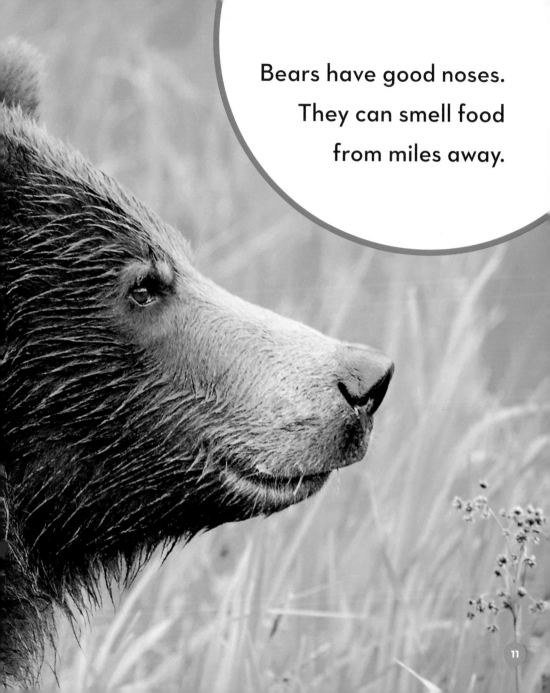

Bears have good noses.
They can smell food
from miles away.

Some bears sleep all winter. They do not get up until spring.

FOOD

In the wild, bears hunt for food. At zoos, bears are given plants and meat to eat.

BEAR CUBS

Young bears are called cubs. Cubs live with their mothers for at least one year.

BEAR FUN

Cubs play together. They learn about hunting.

Most bears
can swim.
They swim
to cool off.

21

FAST FACTS

- Bears can stand up on their **hind** legs.

- Black bears can run up to 35 miles (56 km) per hour.

- There are eight **species** of bear.

- A polar bear can smell a seal on the ice up to 20 miles (32 km) away.

QUICK QUIZ

1. Bears can smell food from miles away. *True or False?*

2. All bears sleep in the winter. *True or False?*

3. Bear cubs live with their mothers for at least one year. *True or False?*

4. Most bears can swim. *True or False?*

GLOSSARY

hind – located in the back or rear.

mammal – a warm-blooded animal that has hair and whose females produce milk to feed their young.

species – a group of related living beings.